I0171924

Christmas Rediscovered!

Unwrapping Your Gift

by

Carolyn Priester Jones

^

Mountjoy
Press

Copyright © 2024 by Carolyn Priester Jones

All rights solely reserved by the author. The author guarantees all contents are original and do not infringe on the legal rights of any other person or work. No part of this book may be reproduced in any form without the permission of the author.

Unless otherwise indicated, Bible quotations are taken from:

THE HOLY BIBLE, NEW INTERNATIONAL VERSION® (NIV2011). Copyright © 1973, 1978, 1984, 2001, 2005, 2011 by Biblica, Inc. ™ (formerly International Bible Society). www.zondervan.com

Scripture quotations are from the ESV® Bible (The Holy Bible, English Standard Version®), copyright© 2001 by Crossway Bibles, a publishing ministry of Good News Publishers.

Holy Bible, New Living Translation, copyright ©1996, 2004, 2015 by Tyndale House Foundation.

The Living Bible, copyright © 1971 by Tyndale House Foundation.

New King James Version (NKJV) are from THE HOLY BIBLE: NEW KING JAMES VERSION. Copyright 1982 by Thomas Nelson Inc.

Amplified® Bible (AMP), Copyright © 2015 by The Lockman Foundation. www.lockman.org

Some scriptures have adjusted capitalization, punctuation, or word order for emphasis. However, the meaning of the scripture has not been altered.

In all cases, I encourage the reader to use the scripture reference to read the Bible verses in their preferred translation, while seeking the guidance of The Holy Spirit for its true message.

CONTENTS

INTRODUCTION

My perceptions of Christmas have changed over the years.

When I was little, Christmas had a lot to do with a jolly, fat man, who was expected to come down our chimney while I slept.

I hoped I had been good enough to be rewarded with the presents I had asked him to give me.

As I got older, some of my friends broke the news that there really was no Santa. I was crushed.

When I confronted my mother about what I saw as a major deception, she simply smiled and said, "Oh they just don't understand. Santa is the spirit of Christmas. He's all about the joy of giving."

Her simple explanations held me for a few more years. Gradually I came to understand. Even if Santa was not real in the way I first imagined him, he was indeed about the joy of giving.

My parents loved giving and of course, I loved receiving. In later years I was able to sneak some presents under the tree to them from Santa. We all celebrated with no doubts expressed of where the gifts came from.

As time went on, I began to associate Christmas with the decorations, lights and pageantry.

Christmas was a time of connecting with others, whether it was through Christmas cards or letters or getting together in person.

Christmas became a time of solidifying long held family traditions and introducing new ones. That included our religious traditions.

The telling again of the Christmas story, singing familiar Christmas carols and sharing candle lit Christmas Eve services were sources of comfort and joy.

In a world gone progressively mad, having times of celebration of Love, Joy and Peace brought hope.

Then I became a Mom. I was back into the world of

Santa again. I got to experience the fresh wonder of seeing Christmas through a child's eyes.

But the time came when the Christmas experience changed again. The daughter grew up and moved far away. Parents, in laws, some family and close friends were promoted to heaven.

Christmas lost its sparkle for me. I began to feel the effects of its commercialization. In contrast to sermons and songs about Peace on earth, peace on earth was getting harder to find.

People began arguing over how to greet one another during the Christmas season. Many expressed concern that Christ was being taken out of Christmas.

But the real problem seemed deeper than how we were going to communicate with each other.

The real problem was we had forgotten how to remain connected with The Living God throughout all seasons of life.

I began a personal journey to reconnect with God in every moment. But I still wanted to know how God intended Christmas to be celebrated.

God said,

Call to Me
and I will answer you
and tell you great and unsearchable
things you do not know.
Jeremiah 33:3

So I asked Him. He answered! And what an adventure He had in store for me.

Through an amazing series of events, what started as a simple personal search became a book called *Christmas of Discovery*, which is still marketed today around the world.

That journey did not stop with one season. It became a continuing discovery of God's Gifts and a revelation of how very present He is in every moment.

And now, as we begin another Christmas season, it is time to share new insights and discoveries.

I invite you to join me as we revisit the birth of Jesus and look at how He reveals Himself today. You will also get a bit of reminiscence that may prompt you to take your own journey to Christmas past.

And sprinkled in, there are some playful grins and giggles. You may even have the urge to sit down, have some cookies and milk, and let go with a few "Ho, ho, ho's!"

DEDICATION

I dedicate this Life and this book to The Creator of the Joy and Music in my life — my Father God.

I praise God and thank Him for walking with me and talking with me. I thank Him for giving me the Words of this book. I thank Him for all the other lessons He has taught me. I thank Him for allowing me to be His "why" child and ask Him unending questions. I thank Him for forgiving me and allowing too many "do overs" to count. I love our life together. I look forward to an Eternity of sharing our Love!

Carolyn Priester Jones

September 25, 2024

ACKNOWLEDGEMENTS

I thank God for putting me in a family who made it easy to understand God's Love and Grace.

I thank God for His Pure Love revealed in all the seasons He gave my parents, Horace and Pearl Priester.

I thank God for giving me a true soulmate in Jay Jones, my husband of 47 years. Using his gift of added dimension, Jay constantly shows me the wonders of God's World. His creativity and ingenuity continue to amaze me.

Jay and I have been partners in teaching, video production and writing books. This book, as well as numerous other projects, would not have come to life without Jay.

Someone once said of us, "She dreams it up, but he makes it happen."

I am blessed to be married to Jay, who makes my dreams come true!

Chapter One
SEEING JESUS

In this season of lights and activities, we may be entertained. But we may also get distracted from the real reason for the season.

When our daughter was three years old, she taught me an important lesson about focusing on Jesus.

I had a nativity set. I very carefully placed the shepherds, the wise men, and all the animals in orderly array around the little baby Jesus.

Every time our daughter was in the room, she carefully moved all the figurines into a tight bunch around the baby Jesus.

I just as carefully moved them back, cautioning her to "look, but don't touch." However, somehow the figurines kept finding their way back into the tight huddle.

Finally, in exasperation, I asked our daughter why she

kept moving them.

She looked genuinely puzzled, as she said, "Mommy, if they don't get close, they can't see Jesus!"

I got the Message, sent by God, through His precious little one. Jesus is here, ready to celebrate with us. But we have to get close to see Him.

I invite you to nose up to the manager, as close as you can get and see Jesus. His Smile will melt your heart!

> *His Mouth is sweetness itself;*
> *He is altogether lovely ...*
> *Song of Songs 5:16*
>
> *... His Face was like the sun*
> *shining in all its brilliance.*
> *Revelation 1:16*

Chapter Two
GOD'S PLANNED PARENTHOOD

Jesus' birth was expected. It was foretold by prophets long before it happened.

But Jesus' birth was not expected by those who would be most involved in making the prophecy come to life.

Both Mary and Joseph were told of the forthcoming miracle. Both were told through what Power a remarkable Life would be brought forth.

The angel told Mary,

> *"The Holy Spirit will come upon you,*
> *and the power of The Most High will overshadow you;*
> *therefore the child to be born*
> *will be called holy—*
> *The Son of God."*
> *Luke 1:35*

Joseph was told,

"Do not be afraid
to take Mary home as your wife,
because what is conceived in her
is from The Holy Spirit."
Matthew 1:20

Paul told us,

"Do you not know
that your bodies are temples of The Holy Spirit,
Who is in you,
Whom you have received from God?
You are not your own."
1 Corinthians 6:19

The Christmas story tells us not all pregnancies are expected by us, but they are always expected by The One Who created the life.

The Christmas story tells us about choice. God chooses to create. He chooses to whom He will give gifts yet unopened or even recognized.

He waits for His Gifts to be opened, received with Joy, and shared with the world.

Before I formed you
in your mother's body
I chose you.
Jeremiah 1:5

For we are God's Masterpiece.
He has created us anew in Christ Jesus,
so we can do the good things
He planned for us long ago.
Ephesians 2:10

Chapter Three
WHAT MARY KNEW

Mary was a young lady whose life had turned upside down.

By all accounts, Mary had grown up in a good Jewish home, following all the proper Jewish traditions. It may have seemed to her that her life was somewhat predictable.

Learn the lessons from your parents, obey, grow up well, meet a nice boy, have a marriage arranged or at least approved by your parents, be a good wife, have children and grandchildren, die, and go to heaven.

Mary had fulfilled all the first parts of the plan. She was now engaged to Joseph. BUT ... while God knew the Plan He had for Mary, He had not yet told her.

You may believe you know the Plan for your life. In fact, even now, you may be working diligently toward creating the picture you have in your mind of what your life should be.

But there is Someone Else Who is working to create a beautiful picture of your life. God is even now fulfilling the Plan He has for you!

> *"For I know the Plans I have for you,"*
> *declares the Lord,*
> *"Plans to prosper you*
> *and not to harm you,*
> *plans to give you hope and a future."*
> *Jeremiah 29:11*

While Mary was planning her life, an angel appeared to her and said,

> *"Greetings,*
> *you who are highly favored!*
> *The Lord is with you."*
> *Luke 1:28*

How would you respond to such a greeting? I believe I would have been more concerned about the presence of someone I did not know, talking to me.

Luke 1:29 reports:
Mary was greatly troubled at his words

and wondered what kind of greeting this might be.

Could it be Mary was concerned that if the Lord was present and He had found her to be highly favored, He might expect something from her? Something that would interfere with her plans? I'm betting she had no idea how far from her plans the Plans of God were.

The angel continued:

> ..."*Do not be afraid,*
> *Mary; you have found favor with God."*
> *Luke 1:30*

There it was again. She was favored by the Lord! The angel went on to give her some details of The Plan. She was to become the mother of Jesus. And the angel told her Who Jesus was.

> "*He will be great*
> *and will be called The Son of The Most High.*
> *The Lord God will give Him*
> *the throne of His Father David,*
> *and He will reign over Jacob's descendants forever;*
> *His Kingdom will never end."*
> *Luke 1:32-33*

Notice the angel did not offer Mary a choice of whether she would like to do this. He simply told her what was about to happen. He then gave her other details about her Aunt Elizabeth's pregnancy in her old age.

The angel ended with a simple statement,

> *"For no Word from God will ever fail."*
> *Luke 1:37*

When God calls us to a task, He does not take it back because of our reluctance. He does not take it back because we doubt. He does not take it back because we are quite sure such an outrageous thing could never happen to us. He calls and waits for us to respond.

With Mary's response, the curtain between heaven and earth began to separate. All the angels and saints of God heard Mary's answer and they began to sing the Hallelujahs that are still heard around the world. What did Mary say?

> *"I am The Lord's Servant,"*
> *Mary answered.*
> *"May Your Word to me be fulfilled!"*
> *Luke 1:38*

Can you say the same thing about everything God has planned for you?

Chapter Four
JOSEPH, DID YOU KNOW?

While we meditate on what Mary knew about Jesus, I wonder about Joseph.

Even if Mary had been willing to accept God's Plan for her life, what if Joseph had not been willing to accept this very unexpected pregnancy?

At the heart of marriage is God's common call to both people. So God did not give the remarkable call to Mary without confirming it to Joseph.

But before Joseph heard news from an angel, he got other news from Mary. That news was shocking ... and devastating.

Joseph was sure he was going to marry a Godly woman. Now here she was, pregnant. And Joseph was quite sure he was not the father.

We don't know what conversations took place between Mary and Joseph when she knew. Did he ask her who the father was? Did Mary tell him? Did he believe her?

Did he wonder how The Holy Spirit could impregnate his future bride? Did the thought of The Holy Spirit make him feel afraid he had somehow stumbled into an alien world?

All Joseph wanted to do was run away... divorce Mary quietly... and try to regain the predictable life he had.

Matthew 1:19 records

> *Because Joseph her husband*
> *was faithful to the law,*
> *and yet did not want to expose her*
> *to public disgrace,*
> *he had in mind to divorce her quietly.*

And then the angel came. The angel told Joseph,

> *"Do not be afraid to take Mary home*
> *as your wife,*
> *because what is conceived in her*
> *is from The Holy Spirit."*
> *Matthew 1:20*

Joseph heard again what Mary had already told him.

The Father of Mary's child was THE Father ... his Father God.

In that moment, Joseph knew that not only had Mary been chosen by God, but he also had been chosen. He was to raise The King of Kings.

Joseph must have wondered, "Can a man raise God?"

The angel continued.

> *"She will give birth to a son,*
> *and you are to give Him*
> *The Name Jesus,*
> *because He will save His people*
> *from their sins."*
> *Matthew 1:21*

Was Joseph's head spinning by now? A boy ... a man ... who could forgive sins? Only God could do that.

The angel made it sound like his marrying Mary and becoming the responsible father of this extraordinary baby was a done deal.

And it sounded like the child's "biological" Father had already picked the name.

Joseph said the name a few times.
"Jesus ... Jesus ... Jesus."

Each time He said it, he felt himself becoming more sure. He didn't know exactly what he was signing on for, but he knew he wanted to be with Mary and Jesus forever.

The tender moment of Joseph's proposal to Mary was not recorded. But I like to think it was on a star lit night where a certain star was beginning to grow brighter.

The breeze that caressed both their faces was The Spirit, Who sang a sweet lullaby to the baby growing inside Mary.

Chapter Five
A DIFFERENT NATIVITY SCENE

The Bible tells us Jesus was God, but He was also human in every way that counts. God chose to live the full picture of being human.

And young Mary and Joseph were definitely human.

We often picture a nice Hallmark card nativity scene. Mary and Joseph have every hair in place. Their clothes are clean. They look happy and peaceful.

We buy into the Away In A Manger song that says, "The little Lord Jesus, no crying He makes." The Bible does not say that at all. He likely cried like any other baby.

He needed his diapers changed. He needed to be fed. He needed to be burped.

Mary had just endured a journey while being close to time to deliver. With a crowd of people headed for Bethlehem for the census, it is likely they made their journey in plenty of traffic. Were they worried about whether they would get there before she delivered?

I wonder how many questions Mary and Joseph had to answer about the unusual pregnancy. We never hear that side of the story. Was there gossip? Was there finger pointing and judgement? Was there curiosity about how such a thing had happened?

And once they got to where they were going, how did Mary and Joseph feel about ending up with the animals? Did they have any thoughts that a very pregnant woman deserved some better accommodations?

But perhaps Mary and Joseph were so tired, they may have been grateful to bunk in with the animals away from the noise of prying people.

And what about the birth itself? If everything went according to human scenarios, Mary had labor pains. We don't know for how long.

If Jesus was not spared the pain of crucifixion, it is unlikely Mary would have been spared the pain of childbirth.

Did Joseph deliver Jesus? Did an unnamed relative

help? Were the animals in the way? Who cleaned up after the birth?

Even though it might shake up our picture perfect nativity scene, it is possible Jesus' first cries were heard by his exhausted parents lying in uncomfortable, itchy hay with the smell of animal excrement in their nostrils.

Why even think of it this way? Because Jesus comes to us in our very real world of unexpected joys and sorrows. He comes to us when life isn't working like we planned.

He comes to us when our backs are against the wall and we don't know what we are going to do next.

He comes to us in our pain, in our questioning of why we have to have pain. He pushes on us and then gives us moments to rest.

He tears through our defenses and bursts into our world whether we are ready or not.

He comes to us in our exhaustion and in the middle of our messes. He cries, He poops, He pees with us.

But He also smiles, laughs and reaches out and touches our face, like we are the most special people in His World.

He doesn't care whether we look picture perfect or not. He sees us as we are and He loves us. He has come to stay.

I wonder what Jesus was like as a toddler. What was His First Word? Do we maybe have no record of his toddler antics because Mary was too tired to record anything after running after Him all day? (Toddler mothers will understand.)

> *Since therefore the children share*
> *in flesh and blood,*
> *He Himself likewise partook*
> *of the same things...*
> *He had to be made like His brothers*
> *in every respect.*
> *Hebrews 2:14 and 17*

Jesus came to be like us so He can reveal to us how much we are like Him!

Chapter Six
THE FIRST EVANGELISTS

We do not know their names.

We do not know how many there were.

They were workers, just faithfully doing their jobs one night when their world was completely upended.

They were some of the first to see Jesus up close and personal.

After that, we do not know how many people they told about Jesus. They disappeared back into anonymity, but The Name of Jesus is known everywhere today.

Those first evangelists may be unknown to us, but Jesus knew them well. He identified Himself as one of them.

He said, "I am The Good Shepherd;
I know My sheep and My sheep know Me."
John 10:14

Those who were called shepherds were also sheep in the care of The Good Shepherd. And on one special night, He gave them a front row seat in Glory.

By all accounts, the shepherds were just having a regular work night taking care of the sheep.

There is no indication they expected anything different. But God had a surprise for them.

> *An angel of The Lord appeared to them,*
> *and The Glory of The Lord shone around them.*
> *Luke 2:9*

The shepherds were terrified.

But the angel said to them,

> *"Do not be afraid.*
> *I bring you good news*
> *that will cause great joy for all the people.*
>
> *Today in the town of David*
> *a Savior has been born to you;*
> *He is The Messiah, The Lord.*
>
> *This will be a sign to you:*
> *You will find a baby wrapped in cloths*

and lying in a manger."
Luke 2:10-12

This in itself would be a lot to digest, but before the shepherds could call a time out, God brought in His Reinforcements.

Suddenly a great company
of the heavenly host
appeared with the angel,
praising God and saying,
"Glory to God in the highest heaven,
and on earth peace to those
on whom His Favor rests."
Luke 2:13-14

Can you imagine what it must have been like to be surrounded by a great company of angels praising God?

Can you imagine being a part of that great chorus? Perhaps even the sheep sang!

Can you imagine Peace on earth really seeming possible, for even a few minutes?

Can you imagine yourself as favored by God to receive such a special birth announcement?

How would you respond?

The shepherds knew immediately what they wanted to do.

When the angels had left them
and gone into heaven,
the shepherds said to one another,
"Let's go to Bethlehem
and see this thing that has happened,
which The Lord has told us about."

So they hurried off
and found Mary and Joseph,
and the baby,
who was lying in the manger.
Luke 2:15-16

We don't know how long the shepherds stood in awe at the manger. We don't know if Mary let them hold the little baby Jesus as tenderly as they held their littlest lambs.

We don't know if they visited more than once. But we do know what they did when they went back into the world.

They shared the good news. God has come to us on earth!

When they had seen Him,
they spread the word
concerning what had been told them about this child,
and all who heard it were amazed
at what the shepherds said to them.
Luke 2:17-18

Chapter Seven
WHAT MADE THE WISE MEN WISE?

I have always wondered about things. I want to know more than what is told in the story.

I wonder about those wise men and their gifts.

How did they decide what to give Jesus?

Did they think about it ahead of time?

Did they discuss who was bringing what? (I mean, usually people sign up for the potluck, so we don't all bring mashed potatoes).

What was the real significance of their gifts? There has been a lot of speculation, but does anyone really know?

What do we know about the wise men?

Why do we remember them as wise?

Can we learn anything from them?

Only the gospel of Matthew mentions them. Many assume there were three because three gifts are mentioned. But Matthew did not say there were only three.

He did not say they were kings. It is rather more likely they were just men who studied the stars.

The wise men were looking up when they saw the star.

They were not content to just say, "Look at that!" And see if it happened again. They took action.

They sought to learn more, even when they did not know exactly what they were seeking.

They followed where God led them, even when they did not know where they were going.

They were persistent. Even though it took a long time, they kept going. It is likely they did not even arrive until a couple of years after Jesus' Birth.

Presented with whether to listen to an earthly king or a heavenly king, they made the right choice. They listened to God.

And when they finally found Jesus, they gave Him their best Gift first. They fell down and worshipped Him.

I wonder how long they stayed. I wonder how Jesus The Toddler reacted to them. I wonder what Mary and Joseph did with their gifts.

I wonder how many people they told about their encounter with The Lord of The Universe.

I wonder if they came back to visit again.

One thing is certain. They went away changed. And when they looked up forever afterwards, they understood what David The Psalmist meant when he said,

"The heavens declare
The Glory of God!"
Psalm 19:1

They had seen God in All His Glory up close and personal!

For The Lord gives wisdom;
from His Mouth
comes knowledge and understanding.
Proverbs 2:6

Chapter Eight
TOUCHED BY JESUS

Have you ever been touched by Jesus? I have. His healing touch came through the tiny hands of our fourteen month old grandson, Gideon.

Gideon was a typical toddler. He explored every inch of the world around him, looking, listening, touching, feeling, tasting and more.

Before one of his visits, I scraped my arm, resulting in a large, painful skin tear.

Later when I was holding Gideon, his little fingers zeroed in on my broken skin.

I instinctively started to pull away. Then I realized he was gently exploring.

He stopped and laid his hand over the wound and was still for a few moments.

Warmth came from his hand. To my amazement, the

pain stopped. I felt peaceful. I felt trust in this little one who touched me with love.

It was a few moments' interaction, but so powerful. My arm began to heal from that minute on.

It prompted me to wonder what the touch of baby Jesus was like. We always imagine Jesus as coming to power at the time of His public ministry. But what about the times before He became known as a healer?

When His baby fingers touched Mary and Joseph, did they feel The Power?

When the shepherds and wise men came, did they get to touch Him? Did the animals experience the warmth of His Touch and feel at peace?

And now, as we celebrate the birth of Jesus, have we reached out in faith and touched Him? Have we let Him touch us and heal our wounds?

Take a few moments. Nose right up to that manger and let Him touch you. Feel The Power of a Love far greater than you can imagine!

Moved with compassion,
Jesus reached out with His hand
and touched him,
and said to him,
"I am willing; be cleansed."
Mark 1:41

Chapter Nine
WHO DO YOU SEE IN THE MANGER?

If you could nose up to the manger and look at the baby Jesus, what do you suppose you would see?

A creative minister once invited people to come and see Jesus in the manger. As people filed by, they gasped in astonishment.

What was in the manger was a mirror. They saw themselves.

Would it surprise you if you saw yourself?

Not the self others see.

Not the self you have come to see.

But the you who once came from your mother's womb ... new ... fresh ... innocent ... unaware of evil ... free of sin ... trusting of those who would take care of you.

Would you like to be that way again?

You can.

That is the true meaning of Jesus' Words,

> *"You must be born again."*
> *John 3:7*

He was saying, "By The Power of The Holy Spirit that is in you, you can begin a new life. Come. Let Me show you how I see you."

Look in that manger again.

See Jesus. See Him in you!

> *On that day, you will realize that*
> *I am in you and you are in Me!*
> *John 14:20*

> *I praise You because*
> *I am fearfully and wonderfully made;*
> *Your Works are wonderful,*
> *I know that full well.*
> *Psalm 139:14*

Chapter Ten
GROWN UP JESUS

What if every year when it is close time for your birthday, we got excited because you were about to be born?

What if we had a whole season devoted to your soon coming arrival on earth?

What if we pulled out from an attic somewhere your first basinet and put a picture of you as a new born in it?

Wouldn't that sound a little strange?

Would you be trying to get someone's attention to say, "I am already here! I have been here forever! Look at me!"

And yet every year we seem to do that to Jesus. We spend a season anticipating His Birth.

We sometimes change "God with us" into "God comes

and goes with the seasons."

When Christmas is over, we box Jesus up until we enter a season of mourning because we are about to focus on His death.

We briefly truly celebrate His Resurrection, only to box Him up again until Christmas.

Jesus is not seasonal. He is God with us always. He is fully grown and waiting for us to grow up enough to celebrate Him fully.

Jesus said,

*"On that day you will realize that
I am in My Father, and you are in Me,
and I am in you!"*
John 14:20

I am with you always. Be sure of this!
Mathew 28:20

You don't have to wait until December 25th to welcome Jesus. He is already here. And He is here to stay.

That knocking you call your heartbeat is Him knocking to remind you He's with you every moment.

Now that is a reason to celebrate!

Joy to the world. The Lord has come!

Chapter Eleven
WHERE IS JESUS TODAY?

If we were an observer from another planet, we might agree that humans reach a whole new level of strange behavior that defies explanation during what we call the Christmas season.

The following is the report of an alien scout to his commander.

This is the strangest place I have yet visited. As you know, you sent me to earth to observe humans during what they call the Christmas season.

Since you sent me here at the height of what is supposed to be the most joyous season, I had great hopes of seeing a level of Peace and Joy that might even exceed that on our planet.

So far, peace and joy seem in short supply.

The life forms here apparently limit some of the most joyful music to only certain times of the year. To play their "December music" in any other month but late November or December is considered unusual.

Their Christmas music is a very odd assortment. They play songs every year sung by people who died years ago. I have not actually seen these dead people in the flesh.

But they have somehow captured and preserved their likenesses and voices. It's a little creepy, but we might want to explore how they are doing this.

They play these Christmas songs everywhere, on radios, on TVs, in stores, even on the streets. Even those seeking shelter in their own homes are often sought out, so they can be exposed to the music. I think it may be a form of mind control.

The music seems to affect humans differently. Some seem happy and even peaceful. Some seem agitated.

I've looked for some of the ones they sing about. But so far I have not been able to identify them.

These humans seem to truly honor reindeer. They have reindeer statues on their lawns. They sing about one with a red nose. He seems to have been a real hero.

I tried to get a glimpse of these creatures by waiting at a place where they are supposed to cross the road. It was clearly marked "deer crossing," but these creatures must be quite independent. None ever came. I shall continue to look.

The humans also put a lot of emphasis on someone they call Santa Clause. At first I thought he was the head reindeer, but he apparently is some advanced human life form.

He can do things other humans cannot do. He apparently cannot fly himself, but he commands some of the reindeer who can fly.

He has some magic power that all the thicker humans wish they had. He eats constantly, mainly a diet of cookies and milk. He is rather thick around the middle but is able to deflate himself and be skinny enough to slide down chimneys.

The humans hold him in such high esteem that they dress like him and give gifts in his name.

I have also noted another very puzzling practice of these life forms. They decorate their houses inside and out during the Christmas season. But as soon as the season ends and it is the darkest time of the year, they turn off the lights and take down the decorations. Very strange indeed.

They also argue a lot about what is a proper way to greet each other in this season. Instead of just saying "hello," they insist on a special greeting during the season.

Some insist on saying, "Merry Christmas" while others say, "Happy Holidays." Both sound pretty close to what they call "merry" here, but apparently the argument has something to do with a baby named Jesus.

I have tried to research Him, since apparently He also fits somewhere in this season on planet earth.

I asked many humans about Him. Many were too busy to answer me. Some tried to explain. They often used the same phrases, but I did not understand.

I asked a small human if she knew where to find out more and she said the strangest thing of all. She told me to ask Him directly.

When I asked her where to find Him, she told me He

was in my heart. I don't understand.

Can you send me further instructions?

Who is this Jesus? How do I find Him?

In due time the scout received an Answer. It didn't come from the planet commander.

It came from The Grand Commander of The Universe.

I AM called
Wonderful Counselor,
Mighty God,
Everlasting Father,
Prince of Peace.
Isaiah 9:6

I AM The Alpha and The Omega,
Who is, and
Who was, and
Who is to come,
The Almighty.
Revelation 1:8

You will seek Me and find Me
when you seek Me with all your heart.
Jeremiah 29:13

And so it was that the scout learned about Love, Joy and Peace ... and the true meaning of Christmas.

Chapter Twelve
THE GIFT THAT KEEPS ON GIVING

This is the season of gift giving. Do you give gifts? Do you like receiving them?

I have given and received many gifts over the course of my life. I have learned these lessons.

Never give a gift out of obligation. If you are only giving because you think you have to, the joy is already draining out.

Never give a gift whose cost is based on what you got or think you might get from the intended recipient.

Never give a gift of something you really want but is not what the other person wants. Suspend the way you think and see the world through the recipient's eyes. What would be precious to them?

Never delay giving a gift until it is a certain day on the calendar. The recipient may need that joy now.

Don't stop giving gifts when the season is over. Many people suffer from the post-Christmas doldrums in January. They may need a gift then.

Don't turn your gifts into a performance test of what a good gift giver you are. I once had a friend who insisted on giving me clothes very year and then routinely checked to see if I was wearing them and asked me again and again if I really liked them.

Don't feel like any gift is a loss. You receive some gifts because God is going to give you the joy of giving it to someone else. You may not need it or want it, but someone else does.

Don't over obsess about wrapping your gift in the most expensive wrapping paper and bows. They will be torn off in minutes and go in the trash.

Don't think a temporary smile or squeals of glee over a gift equals true long-lasting happiness or love. Neither happiness nor love can be bought.

Don't think all gifts can be held in your hands. Some of the most precious gifts are intangible.

So if those are the don'ts, what are the do's?

Take your cues from The Master Gift Giver Himself — God.

He gave The Gift of Himself as a vessel of Love.

He put Himself inside the wrapping of Jesus. When that wrapping was torn off, it revealed a Gift that would bring more than just a smile. It brought Pure Love here to stay forever.

He did not give just to those who chose Him. He gave Himself to every creature in heaven and on earth.

He gave Himself to those on both the naughty and the nice list.

He gave Himself to those who were so lacking in love they didn't even know it was really what they wanted and needed most.

He gave freely. It was a Gift, not a transaction.

He did not wish the recipients a Merry Christmas and leave. He did a truly remarkable thing.

He agreed to be wrapped up again in a different wrapping and be given as a Gift to those who may not have opened The Gift when He first gave it to them.

He wrapped Himself in you. He is ready to be given again and again.

Ask Him where you will be going to deliver the best Gift anyone will ever receive.

And thank Him for The Joy that comes each time you give The Gift that keeps on giving!

The Gift of God is Eternal Life
in Christ Jesus our Lord!
Romans 6:23

Chapter Thirteen
THE BEST GIFT YOU CAN GIVE

My parents lived a life of gratitude. Any time we asked them what they wanted for Christmas, they would answer, "Just your love."

It was enough for them to live a life where they loved God, and they knew He loved them ... and they loved others and knew they were loved.

Jay's parents also lived a life of gratitude. When we asked Jim, Jay's Dad, how he was doing, he would smile and say, "I am fine. I have a great sufficiency!"

We exchanged gifts on Christmas Day, but they were usually simple, inexpensive, and spoke to our knowing each other well. We knew what would make each other smile.

It might be a bottle of old spice aftershave for Daddy, a box of Whitman's Sampler candy for mother, a new piece of sheet music for me ... and always with love notes included.

And we talked. There were no cell phone interruptions, no ducking off to watch tv. We were truly with each other, looking at each other, remembering our past, celebrating our present and anticipating our future.

Our real present to each other was our truly being present with each other.

In sadness, some have shared how some celebrations now are merely extensions of parallel living.

Family and friends are physically in each other's space. They can check the box they made it to the get together on a certain day.

They eat the food. They have a little conversation about the state of the world, and maybe share a little about their current lives.

But truth be told, they then often retreat back to their real lives without a clue of how little they really know about each other.

The pandemic of 2020 prompted many to think about the joy of being together.

Now that restrictions have eased up, the question still remains.

If we are together without all of our devices, do we know how to relate to each other in person ... unplugged?

This year, I encourage you to really be present, wherever you are. Really see other people. Be truly thankful for who God created them to be.

Go beyond just waving to your neighbors or leaving cookies on their front porch. Invite them over for a sit-down visit.

Go ahead and send those cards and letters. But consider also making a phone call to begin to connect more.

And don't make your family and friends a seasonal project. Stay in touch all through the year.

Stay connected to Jesus, who is the best example of continued Presence, and let Him show you how to connect with others.

I am with you always!
Matthew 28:20

Chapter Fourteen
SANTA THE MISSIONARY

C hildren are brought up with the idea of asking Santa for things.

They are drawn into the idea that good behavior gets desired rewards.

They are threatened with rejection or punishment by Santa if they mess up.

They are told Santa or one of his elves are watching them all the time, not in love, but to keep score of how they are performing.

And, of course, all this goes on for just a season. After Christmas, Santa and his elves go back to the North Pole. Children have to wait for next year to see him again.

Recently I have noticed how closely these Santa ideas parallel how many see God.

They believe He rewards them for good behavior and abandons them or punishes them for bad behavior.

They believe God or His angels are watching them, not in love, but to keep score. They live with the phrase, "God will get you for that."

And sadly, they do not believe God is with them, except in certain circumstances, and even then, they see Him as doing what He does from a distant location.

Many believe He will not be back until a future time.

Should we eliminate Santa? No!

But what if we used Santa to teach our children about unconditional Love?

What if we taught them about a Loving Presence in their lives who knows what is happening and wants them to behave in a way that will help Santa spread Love and Joy everywhere?

They could be on Santa's team!

What if we let them feel the joy of receiving a gift, even when they have not earned it? What if we taught them what mercy and grace is all about?

What if we taught them they have the superpower of loving other people and forgiving them when they mess up?

What if we confirmed Santa will go away until next year, but God never will?

What if we taught them He is with them always, loving them and guiding them in the right way?

And finally, what if we encouraged them to pray for Santa and give thanks for His faithfulness and Love?

One of my favorite pictures of our grandson from last year makes it appear he was praying for Santa. I don't know for sure what was being shared between Santa and this precious child.

Perhaps Santa realized this child was not there just to ask for things. He was there to invite Santa into The Kingdom of Heaven.

Jesus said,
"Let the little children come to Me,
and do not hinder them,
for The Kingdom of Heaven
belongs to such as these."
Matthew 19:14

Chapter Fifteen

THE LIGHT SHINES IN THE DARKNESS ...

J ohn described Jesus this way.

In Him was Life,
and that Life was The Light of all mankind.
The Light shines in the darkness,
and the darkness has not overcome it!
John 1:4-5

Dedicated to those who are lighting the darkness. Names changed to protect their privacy.

Kathy lost her husband only a few short weeks after the cancer was discovered. Through her tears, she packed up his clothes to donate. She was comforted by the thought that his sweater, still fragrant with his after shave, would warm someone in need of warmth.

The Light shines in the darkness,
and the darkness has not overcome it.
John 1:5

Wilma endured a lengthy battle with cancer. She lost parts of her physical body, but none of her soul.

As she decorated her Christmas tree, she said a prayer, not complaining about what she had lost, but praising God for what she still had.

The Light shines in the darkness,
and the darkness has not overcome it.
John 1:5

Jack suffered an earthquake within his heart. As he rode in the ambulance, he asked the paramedics to give a copy of his EKG to his wife ... his way of saying, "My heart still beats for you."

The Light shines in the darkness,
and the darkness has not overcome it.
John 1:5

Jane and Phil got the call they never expected. Both of their vibrant parents were killed instantly in a car accident. They stood in line for hours, not just receiving the comfort of others, but giving comfort in return.

> *The Light shines in the darkness,*
> *and the darkness has not overcome it.*
> *John 1:5*

Fred got a call too. It was from the police. His son would not be coming home for a long time, maybe never. He had been arrested for a murder he committed while high on drugs.

Fred went to the chapel and silently lit a candle. He did not understand, but he placed his Hope in The One Who knows all. In faith, he saw the light flickering in his son's heart.

> *The Light shines in the darkness,*
> *and the darkness has not overcome it.*
> *John 1:5*

Stacy lay in the darkness, covered under a blanket of grief and self-doubt. Her daughter had just been found in her apartment where she had committed suicide.

Stacy wondered why she had missed the signs something was wrong. But then she got up and turned on the light by her bed and did the only thing she knew to do.

She read a bible story they had once read together and she sang a lullaby she had once sang. And moments of peace came like falling snow ... cold, but somehow filled with wonder.

The Light shines in the darkness,
and the darkness has not overcome it.
John 1:5

Julie's husband left her and their four children. He was a minister, who lost his way. She did not know until the end how many things he had done to try to find his way back. But it had now been months and all she knew was he was gone.

She tucked the children in and they all prayed. Then she did what she had done every night. She made sure the porch light was on. And she sat by the window and waited.

The Light shines in the darkness,
and the darkness has not overcome it.
John 1:5

Joe went to the church, not to praise God, but to kill His Servants. They welcomed him, but in his rage and confusion, he killed them anyway.

The police took him to jail. The survivors prayed for him. They forgave him. And Jesus Himself shone through their wounds into the darkness. He joined them in saying, " Father, forgive him. He did not know what he was doing."

> *The Light shines in the darkness,*
> *and the darkness has not overcome it.*
> *John 1:5*

Satan never gives up. He tries every day in every way to bring darkness to the world. But he cannot prevail.

As long as there are people who will hold up even one tiny light to God, He will amplify it many times over. The Light will not only light up the one reaching out in faith, but also the rest of the world.

This is not the season of darkness. It is the season to remember when The Light of The World shines brightly.

Whatever is happening in your life, He is with

you. Look up. Reach up. Hold out your candle and let
Him light it.

When Jesus spoke again to the people,
He said,
"I am The Light of the world.
Whoever follows Me
will never walk in darkness,
but will have The Light of Life."
John 8:12

Chapter Sixteen
PEACE IN THE VALLEY

How do you feel when someone cheerfully tells you to have a Merry Christmas when you feel anything but merry?

There are many reasons why people may not feel joyful.

Some are suffering devastating illnesses or injuries.

Some are grieving the loss of people precious to them.

Some are living in fear and turmoil in unstable homes or even in the midst of war.

Some are homeless or hungry.

What do you do when you don't fit in any of those categories and yet you are not feeling merry? There is every indication you are completely blessed and yet you still feel sad?

Little things annoy you.

You feel like you can't cope with the smallest life problem.

You feel like you have somehow been knocked out of orbit and you are removed from everyone else.

You hate the short days. You feel like you live in a cave. Spring seems years away.

You think of heaven a lot. It sounds good. But you are not there yet. You are here, and it kind of scares you that you want to be there soon.

You are a Christian and so your inability to feel the joy of the season seems like a moral failure.

You thank God He is with you. You apologize for not being joyful.

Depression is a serious problem. It can happen any time, but there are those of us who battle it in the short, dark days of winter.

I tried all kinds of remedies, none of which worked. I cried out to God for help. He began His Response in a very unique way. He gave me tears.

I have Sjorgrens Syndrome. I won't depress you by

recounting all the ways this autoimmune condition can affect a person. But one of them is that your tears dry up. Even when you want to cry, you can't.

As I was reviewing my frustrations (again, in reality, very small compared to what others are enduring), God spoke softly.

He said, "I am here."

He put His Arms around me and cried. Just as Jesus wept with Mary and Martha when they believed Lazarus was dead, He wept with me.

And my long absent tears trickled down my face.

He didn't ask me to come to Him. He came to me. He entered that place of my grief and stayed with me, reminding me again that we are together in whatever happens on earth or in heaven.

I stayed in His Embrace and received His Comfort ... the kind nothing in this world can give.

I received His Peace ... unlike the kind the world tries to give.

For however many minutes, He suspended time. Worries went away. I was still. I knew He was God and I was not.

I felt my powerlessness melt into His Power.

And then I got up, to face another round of winter.

If you are depressed, talk to God about it. He already knows everything you are going through, but He will listen to you tell your story your way.

He will comfort you. He will pour out His Love for you and fill every empty place.

Then listen carefully. He will tell you what to do next.

He is indeed God with you, now and always. He wants you to have real Peace and real Joy — not the manufactured, worldly kind, but the real thing, straight from His Heart to yours.

Peace I leave with you;
My Peace I give you.
I do not give to you as the world gives.
John 14:27

You will show me the path of life.

In Your Presence is Fullness of Joy!

Psalm 16:11

Chapter Seventeen
LET YOUR LIGHT SHINE!

When I was a little girl, my brother gave my parents a very unique Christmas gift. It was a set of ornaments that were supposed to glow in the dark.

The star of this collection was the star. We all waited with great anticipation for the ornaments to kick in and glow.

However, nothing happened. My brother was very disappointed that his gift had bombed.

My mother assured him all the ornaments were lovely in themselves and would be the perfect addition to the tree. He wasn't so sure.

However, one night the miracle happened. Each ornament seemed to glow! Everyone was delighted.

However, unknown to us, my mother had positioned each ornament close to a light on the tree. They appeared to glow on their own, but it was really the reflection of the lights near them.

Many years later, I became the keeper of the ornaments. Each year when I place them on the tree, I think of the lesson Mother subtly taught us.

In ourselves we can do nothing. We have no light of our own to give to this dark world. But when connected to Jesus, The Light of the world, we can shine. We can light up the darkness!

We put the Star on the top of our tree each year. It makes me smile as I see it there. And I can imagine my mother smiling too.

Her ornament is on the tree too. Mother is another word for Love!

I am The Light of the world.
Whoever follows Me
will not walk in darkness,
but will have The Light of Life.
John 8:12

You are the light of the world.
Let your light shine before others,
that they may see your good deeds
and glorify your Father in heaven!
Matthew 5:14 and 16

Chapter Eighteen
THE ROCKET

Christmas does not have to be all serious. Sometimes a little playful mischief is just what is needed to add a little spice.

When I was a little girl, my teenage brother very excitedly brought home something called "the rocket."

It was a device one was supposed to install on their car that would magically increase gas mileage and general efficiency of the car.

Right away my father was skeptical. And sure enough, it turned out to be a dud. He teased my brother unendingly for being taken in.

The rocket disappeared for a while. We probably all assumed my brother had thrown it away. However, the apple does not fall far from the tree. My brother learned practical jokes from my father.

A couple of Christmases later, my father opened his lavished wrapped present with great anticipation. There in its original box was the rocket. My brother felt vindicated in having had the last laugh.

However, the following Christmas, when my brother opened his brightly wrapped present, there, in its original box, was the rocket.

My father and brother kept this up for years, until after my brother was married and becoming a father. The rocket disappeared.

Everyone moved on to the next stages of life, only occasionally enjoying a collective family laugh about the rocket exchange.

When I asked who ended up with the rocket, they both claimed not to remember where the exchange stopped. Neither believed they had it.

Many years passed. Holiday traditions changed. I often was with my in laws in Kentucky for Christmas and we saw my parents in South Carolina for New Years.

But one year we all got together at my brother's house in Georgia for Christmas. By then my parents were in their 90s and my brother was a grandfather.

Everyone enjoyed the gift exchange. Everyone seemed to have gotten their share of gifts. My brother looked a little puzzled as he noticed a small gift tucked under the tree. He fetched it out and read the tag. It was for me.

We all wondered where it had come from and more importantly, from whom. I eagerly dived in to find out.

And there ... in its original box ... was the rocket!

My father laughed and looked at my brother, and said, "You had it!"

My brother insisted he did not have it. And everyone seemed genuinely mystified.

Finally my mother spoke up and said, "Do none of you still believe in Santa?"

It was one of those moments when we all, young and old alike, thought we heard sleigh bells. I was a bit preoccupied because I was already thinking of who I was going to give it to the next year.

So where did it come from? My mother finally confessed. She had been doing some end of life cleaning when she happened upon the rocket.

She said, "All those years you boys were having fun. I thought it was time for us girls to enjoy it now." She winked, as if she was sharing a secret.

It turned out she was. She did not need that rocket to get to her next Christmas. The Lord gave her a much more powerful boost to Heaven.

Where is the rocket today? I'll never tell.

That's part of the mystique. It just appears. And there is laughter and joy … and it creates wonderful Christmas memories!

A joyful heart is good medicine.
Proverbs 17:22

Chapter Nineteen
WHO DIED?

My mother's promotion to Heaven brought many changes to all our lives. She was the organizer, the planner and the glue that kept everything together.

No one could even come close to filling her shoes, but I tried to help my father. Even though he was deep in the grief of having lost The Over 70-year Love of His Life, he wanted to continue with some of their special Christmas practices.

One of them was sending Christmas cards. I agreed to help him.

I thought it would be a relatively simple task. However, we could not find my mother's most current list. We worked from the previous year's list. Right away we hit a snag.

Our conversation went like this.

Me: Let me read through the list and see if we've got everyone you want to send a card to.

I began to read the list. Several names down, he stopped me.

(Names changed in the following scenario to protect the living and the dead)

Daddy: Wait! I think Jack's dead.

Me: OK, I'll take Jack off.

Daddy: But I'm not sure. He was pretty sick and I think he died. But he might have pulled through. If he didn't die, he'd be upset if I didn't send him a card.

Me: OK, I'll put him back on.

Daddy: No wait, what if he did die?

Me: Then he won't get the card.

Daddy: But then his family will know I didn't know he was dead. I wonder if Pearl sent a sympathy card if he died. But then I really don't know who died first ... Pearl or Jack ... if Jack died.

Me: Why don't we send a card to Jack and his wife

and just write a general note that could be taken as an expression of sympathy or season's greetings? Just don't ask him how he is!

Daddy: Yes, that sounds like a good idea.

He picked up his pen to write a note, than paused and looked puzzled.

Daddy: Wait a minute. It's coming back to me now. I think it was Jack's wife, Ann, who was so sick. And I think she died.

Me: OK, then we should take Ann off, but leave Jack on.

Daddy: No, don't do that yet, because I'm not sure. I shouldn't send a card to Jack if he's really the one who died.

Daddy looked very sad at this point.

Daddy: I sure wish your Mama hadn't died. She would know who is dead and alive.

Me: She probably does, Daddy. I wish she was here too. But since she isn't, why don't we just send cards to everyone on the list. Whoever is alive can know we still think of those who have been promoted, as still living.

Daddy seemed satisfied with that. We did get a few back with family explaining who had died and expressing sympathy to Daddy in the loss of my mother.

It was not only Christmas greetings shared that year, but it was also a shared grief. That in itself was comforting.

And Jack really appreciated the Christmas card, since he had just lost his wife, Ann.

It was much easier to help Daddy with his Christmas cards after that first year.

Several years later, after Daddy died in November, he received Christmas cards from people who did not know.

As I wrote them back, I smiled at the precious memories. We all thought of Daddy as still alive. And we were right. He had just had a change of address!

Chapter Twenty
CHRISTMAS LETTERS

I come from a long line of letter writers. Back in what my young friends call "the old days," people put pen to paper and transferred their thoughts into words.

I well remember the joy of receiving mail from relatives and friends, who lived in other places. My father regularly got to see the joy of others receiving mail. He was a mailman, later called a letter carrier.

My parents and their siblings regularly wrote each other. But at Christmas time, my parents wrote letters to a wider audience. They tucked their letters in Christmas cards.

The letters were often a synopsis of the year's activities, a report of current events and well wishes to all for the coming year.

We all eagerly waited for responses from others, who were happy to participate in the same tradition.

When Jay and I got married 47 years ago, I continued the tradition. I began to write an annual Christmas letter. I was always delighted to receive letters from those who were still writing.

We never limited our Christmas list to just those we heard from. It was our joy to remember each and everyone we sent cards and letters to, whether they replied or not.

We liked to think our letters might bring a smile of remembrance that we were once together in whatever way. We liked to believe our thoughts of each other would connect us again.

As I read back over letters from previous years, I began to realize the treasure we had. We had our family's history written through Christmas letters.

I collected them in a book. Perhaps one day, they will bring smiles to someone else, who would like to read about the journey of one family.

Several years ago, God prompted me to add another part to my annual Christmas writing. I prayed specifically for each person to whom we were sending letters.

I knew that The Power of The Holy Spirit released through prayer was the greatest Connector we could have.

In this world of instant everything, letter writing is becoming a dying art. The Christmas season is a perfect time to bring it back. I invite you to try it.

Sit quietly and remember those who contributed to your life. Write them. Thank them. Share your present life.

And know it does not have to be done before any deadline. Take your time. You may find writing a letter a day expressing gratitude, love, joy and peace will be the perfect way to live life through the coming year.

I thank my God every time
I remember you ...
It is right for me
to feel this way about all of you,
since I have you in my heart.
Philippians 1:3 and 7

Chapter Twenty-One
THE CHRISTMAS TREE

The Christmas tree is truly a collage of our life. Each year as I pull the ornaments from the box, I reflect on our journey.

We have ornaments from Jay's family's tree. There are interesting little angels from the 1950s. Each one initially looked the same to me until I discovered a scratch here, a nick there, a broken part here and there – character lines.

LESSON: What happens in life affects who we become, but it does not break us. The scratches, nicks and broken parts can't take away the lasting beauty.

We have ornaments from my family's tree. There is the bird (now rather worn) that clips on to the branch. I remember standing on tip toes to reach it and my mother cautioning, "Gentle touch. Don't knock him off."

LESSON: Be gentle with Life. Life is not a "do not

touch" area, but it should handled with love and a gentle touch.

There is the ornament carefully crafted by my sister-in-law. She took a crafts class one year and outdid herself in creating this beautiful masterpiece. She died unexpectedly the next year. The beauty she created lives on.

LESSON: You are planting seeds for trees under which you may never sit. Plant with enthusiasm seeds that will blossom, even after you are gone.

One of my favorite ornaments is the one given to all the Avon representatives the year Jay became an Avon "person".

One day he came home from a nursing class and announced he had looked around his class, realized that most all of his classmates were female, and that he had the perfect market for cosmetics.

By this time, I was used to his unique approach to life; so I just laughed. But he did become an Avon person and he did have wonderful success. The tree proudly shows the ornament given to all the Avon "ladies."

LESSON: Never put yourself in a box of someone else's making. Learn what it means to have a paradigm shift. See things with an open view and ask, "Why not?!"

Then there are the daughter years. Each year we laugh over the many "Baby's First Christmas" ornaments we received the year she was born.

Since she was born in November, everyone had the same idea for Christmas. And her birth was such an occasion at our house, it was worthy of great celebration.

LESSON: It's impossible to celebrate too much. Run and dance and cheer and give the highest praises to God for His good gifts. The Christmas story tells about one fine celebration! Glory to God IN THE HIGHEST!

There are the multiple ornaments made by our daughter when she was a small child – cardboard, plastic, glitter, pictures that show growing and changing. They all spell love. Tiny hands that were guided by caring teachers and friends into creating ornaments to give Mom and Dad.

LESSON: Love is worth the time it takes to express it. Don't get so caught up in searching commercial avenues for the "perfect" gift. Search your heart instead. Not only Moms and Dads and Grandparents, but also friends would cherish a gift from your HEART to theirs.

I added a heart ornament the year after my mother died. It says "Mother is another word for LOVE."

I called my mother "Mother". She was my best friend, my cheerleader, my adviser, my confidant, my teacher. The last thing she ever said to me in this life was, "I could never forget you. I love you so much."

Her smile seems to fill the room in the glow of the lights, reflecting the love that was an important part of the creation of me ... the love that carried me and held on and let go at all the right times through my life ... the love that still carries me because she is still a part of who I am.

LESSON: Lots of things in life have a beginning and an ending. Love is not one of those things.

Love goes on forever!
1st Corinthians 13: 8

I invite you to reflect on your life.

Think of who you were ... who you are ... and who you will be. Recognize that the elements of who you were and who you are will also be present in who you will be.

If you decorated your tree with mementoes of your life, what would it look like?

Chapter Twenty-Two
SHOULD WE LET SANTA IN?

There was absolutely nothing funny about the real world of COVID. However, as we all spent the Christmas season waiting for life to get better, some of us began to worry about Santa's health.

I wrote this during the Christmas season of 2020.

I went back and read The Night Before Christmas to get a good description of Santa. Now I am concerned.

Have Santa, Mrs. Santa and all those elves been tested for germs? Were they all negative?

Are they all wearing masks? A beard is not an adequate face covering, especially when Santa is spraying who knows what with every Ho, Ho ,Ho.

Who is checking Santa's temperature before he enters a house?

Is Santa already sick? According to the story, "his

cheeks were like roses, his nose like a cherry! His droll little mouth was drawn up like a bow." Sounds like he's got something!

He also apparently can't keep his hands away from his face, especially his nose. Very high risk! The story says, he puts a finger aside of his nose, and we already established his face and nose are red!

Santa sadly has other risk factors that put him in a vulnerable risk group. He is overweight. He apparently eats less than heart healthy food.

He smokes, even on the job. If he exhales that pipe smoke, he may be spreading something.

Are the elves wiping down all the toys with appropri-ate germicide?

Are all those chimneys really clean? In this infectious world, is simple chimney sweeping enough? I think not!

How many people was Santa exposed to, even before Christmas? It looks like, in spite of all the warnings, he was still hanging out at the mall. All kinds of people were in close contact.

And finally, if Santa is masking up, is he in danger of being assaulted by a homeowner, who thinks he is an intruder?

All things considered, should Santa stay home and ship the gifts this year? Just asking … for a friend …

2024 update: Thankfully, in spite of his high risk lifestyle, Santa faithfully made his rounds that year and has continued. We need to look into how he does it. He must have something better than a vaccine!

Chapter Twenty-Three
TOYLAND

I love toys. It was a delight to have a child, so I could legitimately play with toys. But then she grew up. The toys went away.

I did not want to invest in toys for myself when there were no children to enjoy them with me.

Then I met Mary. Mary was a delightful petite bundle of joy, older in years than me, but younger in heart. She knew I liked butterflies, but she did not know of my secret love of toys.

During a time when I was recovering from an illness, she brought me two wind up toy butterflies.

We sat on the floor, wound them up and delighted in the rise and fall of their wings and their journeys around the room.

The joy was back!

And thus began my expanded permission to myself to play and feel joy in various innocent ways. I was no longer constrained by the need to act like an adult.

Then came the ultimate play experience. I became a grandmother! Every time I see my grandson, he teaches me something new about how to enjoy my second childhood.

My childhood joy expands every year to include viewing Christmas lights. I love seeing how people can creatively bring their contributions to the season.

Last year, there were a variety of offerings, but none that touched my heart as much as the hugging teddy bear in a front yard near by.

Set amid a crowd of whimsical inflatables, he opened his arms wide and then gently closed them in a hug.

Last year was a hard season for me with surgical procedures and medical challenges. At various times, I needed a hug.

My family and best friend graciously provided. But additionally the bear reliably gave his hugs. The lights shone brightly through the darkness and the bear beckoned me in.

I decided early in the season the bear's owners should know what mission work they were doing. I determined to contact them before the season was over.

So I wrote them a letter of appreciation, selected my favorite Christmas toy and I gave it to them.

It was an act of faith to just go to the door of strangers on Christmas Eve and deliver a toy. But I must admit I felt like I was a part of Santa's crew.

I was rewarded by warm smiles and exclamations of joy at the receiving. And my favorite toy has a new home!

Never lose the wonder of childhood. Play! Enjoy!

Be open to everyone who will teach you to play, whether they be old or young.

Share the joy. Trust it will light up someone else's world and come back to you!

Jesus came as a Missionary of Joy!

I have told you these things
so that My joy and delight may be in you,
and that your joy may be made full and complete
and overflowing!
John 15:11

Chapter Twenty-Four
WHAT'S IN A NAME?

Names are very important to God.

He even named each star.

David tells us,

> *He counts the number of the stars;*
> *He calls them all by their names.*
> *Psalm 147:4*

God had Adam name the animals.

God named Himself. He told Moses His First Name is I AM.

When God put on human flesh, He revealed His other names.

I AM The Wonderful Counselor.
I AM The Mighty God.
I AM THE Everlasting Father.
I AM The Prince of Peace.
Isaiah 9:6

I AM Immanuel.
I AM God with you.
Matthew 1:23

I AM Jesus!
Matthew 1:21

God revealed even more of Himself through Jesus.

I AM The Bread of Life.
John 6:35

I AM The Light of the world.
John 8:12

I AM The Good Shepherd.
John 10:11

I AM The Resurrection and The Life.
John 11:25

I AM The Way, The Truth and The Life.
John 14:6

I AM The Vine.
John 15:1

I AM The Alpha and The Omega,
I AM The First and The Last,
I AM The Beginning and The End.
Revelation 22:13

But beyond all that, God revealed through Jesus just how much He is God with us. He said the day would come when we knew.

He is inside us. He has called us by name!

I have redeemed you.
I have called you by name.
You are Mine.
Isaiah 43:1

On that day you will realize that
I AM in My Father,
and you are in Me,
and I AM in you.
John 14:20

Look again at the name, Jesus. Find the letter "u." That represents you. You are in Jesus. He is in you.

Now go either to the left or the right of "u." You will find "us." We are together in Jesus and He is in us.

What's in a name? In Jesus, we are!

Chapter Twenty-Five
WHAT DID YOU GET?

After most of the gifts of the season are given, many of us put them away and "survey the loot."

What's the score for true treasures, gifts you might give to someone else as a gift, gifts you hope to learn how to use (gifts to grow into), gifts you may have to change a little before you can use (that sweater that is a tad too snug), and gifts you will save simply because they remind you of the giver?

Are you satisfied with your gifts? What determines how satisfied you are? The answer to that question may, in part, depend upon how much you needed the gift. Consider a gift that literally means Life to you.

One of the most precious experiences of my life was being involved with the Kentucky Organ Donor Affiliates. I signed on for general interest in the cause, not realizing that many of the members are organ recipients themselves.

At the first meeting, I was approached by different people, who asked in an excited hush, "What did you get?"

I thought we were talking about dessert ... until each one began to tell me with awe filled voices what they had received.

Lungs, kidneys, corneas, and other organs ... many recounted with tears in their eyes how they were headed for death and because of a gift of life, they were now healthy and able to tell others about their gift.

We were once headed for death. Sin demands we accept pay for what we have done. This is one time we do not want to be paid for what we did.

The wages of sin is death.
Romans 6:23

If that was the end of the sentence, we would be sitting on death row.

But thank God for His Mercy. He does not want to pay us our just wages. He wants to give us a Gift!

But The Gift of God is Eternal Life
in Christ Jesus our Lord!
Romans 6:23

You can accept your just wages or you can accept a Gift ... the best one you will ever receive ... the Gift of Eternal Life through Jesus Christ our Lord!

Why did Jesus come to earth? The answer was in His Name.

She will give birth to a son,
and you are to give Him the name Jesus,
because He will save His people
from their sins.
Matthew 1:21

Jesus came to deliver The Gift.

Having received so great a Gift, wouldn't you want to tell everyone you knew about it?

How many of us take that Gift and hoard it, reveling in the "I got it" moment ... and forgetting those who don't know the Gift is for them as well.

The beautiful thing about the Gifts of God is when you

give them away, you don't lose them. You gain even more, as Treasures are laid up in Heaven, just waiting for your arrival!

What did you get? Consider the answer to that question with joy! Praise God for His Gifts of Life and pass them on!

Chapter Twenty-Six
THANK YOU FOR THE INTERESTING GIFT!

Do you have regular after Christmas activities? When I was growing up, we all knew what we would be doing the day after Christmas. We would be writing thank you notes.

Not only was my mother very emphatic that we write them, she was also emphatic that we write them soon after we received the gifts.

And she put in another wrinkle. She said we should say how we planned to use it.

Example: "Thank you for the new mixing bowl. You know I love to cook and I plan to bake a chocolate cake this afternoon, using my new mixing bowl."

What if we thought of every gift God has given us and we said, "Thank You, God, for giving me _____. I look forward to using it in this way."

Think of it. "Thank You, God, for our house. I plan to use it in this way." "Thank You, God, for my vision ... my hearing ... etc. I plan to use it in this way."

Have you ever received a gift you did not want or thought you could not use? What could be the purpose in receiving a gift we can't use?

Let's take the example of a child receiving a shirt that is too big, but one that he can grow into and look forward to wearing next year.

Sometimes God's Gifts entice us to wait a little while to use them ... to keep us reaching to the future.

What about the shirt that is too small? What could that teach us? Sometimes it is a gentle reminder we need to change something about ourselves to fit into that nice gift.

Sometimes it is a reminder we have grown. Sometimes we start thinking we are not growing spiritually, and then something comes along that shows us we have grown from where we were last year or even last month.

Sometimes we are given gifts to give to others. I have

received some gifts I never personally used, but I gave them as gifts to others, who really could use them.

God had provided two gifts. One was the gift that went to the person who really needed it. The other was God's Real Gift to me in getting the pleasure of being His delivery girl and sharing in the joy of giving.

When you get a gift you think you will never use, stop a minute and ask God, "Would You like me to deliver this to someone else?"

What about the gift we can't even identify? Everyone in our family still smiles at the memory of gifts from a favorite relative, who never missed giving my parents a gift each Christmas.

The only problem was frequently the gifts were so unique no one knew exactly what they were. A weird-shaped paperweight or a brass apple corer or something none of us could ever identify.

Dutifully after Christmas, my mother would write the thank you letter. However, when you don't know what you have received, it is hard to know how to say thank you! We laughed as we read her thank you notes, which sometimes sounded like this:

"Thank you for the interesting gift. You always put such thought into getting us the perfect gift. We certainly look forward to using it." (And of course, the part that she did not write ... was "when we figure out what it is.")

Sometimes we detect that God has given us gifts, but they were not quite what we expected. However, they often turn out to be wonderful gifts beyond our wildest imagination (once we figure out what they are!).

Accept those gifts with gratitude, thank the Lord for them and wait for their purpose to be revealed.

I invite you to try my mother's principles of writing thank you notes. Think of the gifts God has given you. Thank Him right away. Identify each gift by name and tell Him how you plan to use it.

And if it's some of those gifts you can't quite identify yet, thank God that He knows the Plans He has for you and they are good plans. Look forward to unwrapping those gifts a little bit at a time!

"For I know the Plans I have for you,"
declares The Lord,
"Plans to prosper you
and not to harm you,
Plans to give you hope and a future."
Jeremiah 29:11

Every good and perfect Gift
is from above,
coming down from The Father
of The Heavenly Lights,
Who does not change
like shifting shadows.
James 1:17

Give thanks to The Lord,
for He is good;
His Love endures forever!
1st Chronicles 16:34

Chapter Twenty-Seven
IS THE PARTY OVER?

The Christmas season can be a roller coaster ride. There is so much expectation, so much hype, so much activity, so many highs and so many lows.

By the time Christmas Day has passed, we don't know how to feel. Sometimes we just feel tired. Some may feel sad because it's over or maybe even because it was not all they hoped it would be.

Some feel relieved the season is over. They can hardly wait to get the tree down, decorations boxed up and things returned to "normal."

How does God want us to deal with this some-times-conflicting bundle of after Christmas feelings?

His Answer is simple.

Be still.
Psalm 46:10

God does not mean "Be still and take a long winter's nap." He means "Clear your mind and just be."

Be awake. But have no regrets about the past, no worries about the future, no stressing about this moment.

For a few days at least, and longer if He so directs, be a human being, not a human doing.

Enter The Holy Inner Sanctum of yourself where you will find the best of all Gifts ... The One you may have missed during The Christmas season.

Your body is a temple
of The Holy Spirit within you,
Whom you have from God!
1 Corinthians 6:19

Know that I AM God!
Psalm 46:10

Know that The Almighty God can never be confined to a season, to a manger, to a cross, to a tomb, or even your one body.

Your getting close enough to see Him (See Chapter One) is just the beginning. He has big plans for you and His World.

> *"For I know the plans I have for you,"*
> *declares The Lord,*
> *"plans to prosper you*
> *and not to harm you,*
> *plans to give you hope and a future."*
> *Jeremiah 29:11*

But before you go back out Into the world together, God wants you to understand what He will promise and He wants to know what you will promise in return.

Before we enter the New Year, let's go to a wedding!

Chapter Twenty-Eight
NEW YEAR'S RESOLUTIONS

Many people make New Year's Resolutions. Resolutions are basically promises to ourselves to do better in the New Year.

It is a form of goal setting. It is a way of trying to begin again with a clean slate.

Alas, many of us have broken our resolutions before January is over. We just don't have the will power to control ourselves.

What if we stopped making promises to ourselves and instead entered into marriage Promises with God?

In a marriage the bride frequently puts her husband's name after hers to symbolize their new relationship. In a marriage with God, we get to put His Name first and share in everything He is.

God told Moses His Name is I AM.

God is willing to give us all of Himself. He promises. And He never takes back His Promises.

Before you decide whether you want that close a relationship with God, you might want to know how He feels about you. You might want to hear what He has to offer.

The following chapter verses are taken from the scriptures referenced, but are not direct quotes. The meaning is the same, but I have made them personal as God would speak to you.

I encourage you to also read the direct quote of the scriptures after you read the personalized version.

Chapter Twenty-Nine
WHAT GOD PROMISES YOU

I love you.

I have loved you with an Everlasting Love.
With Unfailing Love, I have drawn you to Myself.
Jeremiah 31:3

I chose you.
John 15:16

I created your inmost being;
I knit you together in your mother's womb.
Psalm 139:13

My Eyes saw your unformed body;
all the days ordained for you were written in
My Book before one of them came to be.
Psalm 139:16

I have redeemed you;
I have called you by name;
you are Mine.
Isaiah 43:1

You are My Masterpiece.
I created you,
so we can do the good things
I planned for us long ago.
Ephesians 2:10

I have come
that you may have Life and
have it to the full.
John 10:10

I want you to be with Me where I am,
and to see My Glory,
The Glory that flows from Love
that started before the creation of the world.
John 17:24

My Peace I give you.
I do not give to you as the world gives.
John 14:27

I have told you this
so that My Joy may be in you
and that your joy may be complete.
John 15:11

I will show you The Path of Life.
In My Presence is Fullness of Joy.
Psalm 16:11

I AM Love.
1 John 4:16

I will always love you.
Jeremiah 31:3

When you receive His Gift of Love, you will also receive His Name. By The Power of His Holy Spirit, once again The Miracle of Life will happen.

You will be able to do that which you could never do apart from Him. When you surrender all of you to all of Him in every moment, you can be assured you are The Living Proof of your marriage.

You will know
I AM Love!

He has promised,

> *"Whatever you ask in My Name*
> *in My Love,*
> *that will I do."*
> *John 14:13*

Chapter Thirty
THE GREATEST GIFT

God is Love. Paul was once a man who did not love.

Then God revealed Himself to Paul up close and personal. And over time, Paul learned what it meant to be loved by God and to let God love others through him.

Paul's description of True Love can be the foundation, not just of our New Year's Promises, but of our New Life Promises.

I encourage you to read all of 1 Corinthians, Chapter 13.

The following joins Paul's description of Love with God's Name, I AM.

Hear God say these Words to you.

Then say them back to Him.

I AM patient.

I AM kind.

I do not envy.

I do not boast.

I AM not proud.

I do not dishonor others.

I AM not self seeking.

I AM not easily angered.

I keep no record of wrongs.

I do not delight in evil.

I rejoice with The Truth.

I always protect.

I always trust.

I always hope.

I always persevere.

My Love for You never fails!

Chapter Thirty-One
GOD IN US

S easons come and go. God stays.

He is as He promised, God with Us.

We are the U in Jesus.

We are the US in Jesus.

We are His Love gifted to us. He is waiting to be unwrapped for all the world to see.

Again Jesus spoke to them, saying,

"I AM The Light of the world.
Whoever follows Me
will not walk in darkness,
but will have The Light of Life."
John 8:12

You are in Me and I AM in you.
John 14:20

You are the light of the world.
Let your light shine before others,
that they may see your good deeds
and glorify your Father in heaven.
Matthew 5:14 and 16

Be sure of this.
I AM with you always!
Matthew 28:20

A Few Imparting Words

I would be blessed to know what you discover as you unwrap The Gift of God in you.

You can email me at:
carolynpriesterjones@gmail.com

Or contact me through my blog site at:
carolynpriesterjones.org

I also invite you to check out my previous books, *Christmas of Discovery* and *If You Only Knew ... Who I AM*. Both are available in print and digitally.

Many Blessings to you and all to whom you will give The Gift.

To Him Who is able to keep you from stumbling
and to present you before His Glorious Presence
without fault and with great joy—
to The Only God our Savior
be glory, majesty, power and authority,
through Jesus Christ our Lord,
before all ages, now and forevermore!
Amen.
Jude 1:24-25

www.ingramcontent.com/pod-product-compliance
Lightning Source LLC
Chambersburg PA
CBHW060806050426

42449CB00008B/1573